Add "*ZING*"
to Your Quest
for Maximum
Success!

Five Steps to Making
Your Vision a Reality

VIC SCHOBER

JONATHAN SCHOBER

ISBN-10: 0996101020
ISBN-13: 978-0-9961010-2-8

DEDICATION

THIS BOOK IS DEDICATED TO TWO OF THE MOST WONDERFUL WIVES THAT A FATHER AND SON COULD EVER HAVE . . . NAOMI AND JENNIFER.. YOUR ENCOURAGEMENT AND POSITIVE AFFIRMATIONS HAVE KEPT US GOING FOR ALL THE YEARS OF OUR MARRIAGES AND WE LOVE YOU DEARLY!

Vic Schober / Jonathan Schober

CONTENTS

Vic Schober / Jonathan Schober

ACKNOWLEDGMENTS

To list the people who have taught us, mentored us, and shared their lives with us to bring us to this place of understanding this process of achieving success through the steps of the ZING are too many to list. Please know that we have many people to whom we owe a great debt of gratitude for being our coaches and examples. Thanks to all of you men and women! We greatly appreciate you!

Vic Schober / Jonathan Schober

PREFACE

HOW MANY TIMES have you seen the need to change or the need for an addition or the need for something new…whether a program or a building or a ministry…but somehow it was never realized? It was a good idea, maybe even a great idea, but…that's all that happened…it was just an idea or a reoccurring thought that never materialized.

Was it good enough to actually have been produced or developed? If so, why wasn't it acted upon? Why didn't it go beyond the "idea" or the "dream"?

Many leaders, pastors, and parents see the need for many things…but somehow that is as far as it goes. Of course, "seeing" is only the beginning of the process…there is much more that must happen in order to bring such a vision into reality.

This book is certainly not an exhaustive study on the topic, but it is a book that hopefully will stir something in every leader, pastor, and parent to want to go beyond simply "seeing" the possibilities. It is the desire of the authors that the contents in each chapter will challenge the spirit in each reader to take on the next step and then the one after that until the project is completed and victory can be claimed.

It is believed that both groups and individuals will benefit by considering the stories and the suggestions that are interwoven into the text of the enclosed chapters. There is a logical process that must be followed to achieve success; and when it is followed, the possibility of "mission accomplished" is almost surely guaranteed.

God wants us to have good success. The Word assures us that we are triumphant; we are more than conquerors; we are the head not the tail; we are meant to be winners not losers!

To have good success requires a process to be developed. As has been said on many an occasion: "It is hard by the yard, but a cinch by the inch." Take on any project and accomplish the goal one step at a time...and eventually those "steps" will add up to a big success.

We trust that these few chapters will stir you into action! If God has given you a dream or a vision, you must articulate it and initiate action, be persistent when you face obstacles, and you will in time put the "finishing touches" on a job well done. Remember this: "With God all things are possible!"

Vic Schober and Jonathan Schober

VISUALIZING: *Seeing* Your Ultimate Goal

VisualiZing: To form a mental image of something not visual to the sight.

LEADERS DON'T CREATE GOALS, THEY CREATE VISION.

When I was 13 years old, I had the opportunity to attend the 1984 World's Fair in New Orleans, Louisiana. The featured exhibit of the expo was the Space Shuttle Enterprise. I was a kid who loved space and the shuttle program was fascinating to me. However, that's not the exhibit that I have the most profound memories of.

There was a room in a small building with a wall of T.V.s that looked like you were walking onto the command center of the Star Trek Enterprise. There was a computer console that you could use to pull up different news and sports stories. The **visionaries** of exhibit were able to *visualize* what we would come to know 10+ years later as "The Internet." *(In fact, 10 years later, I was building my first websites and teaching*

people how to spell "W-W-W".)

WITHOUT A VISION...THE PEOPLE PERISH

I'm in the process of goal setting for the coming year right now. Over the years I've used several methods for goal setting. In the end many of these methods have boiled down to a simple task list. Unfortunately by about the middle of January I'm not longer motivated and the task list just bores me, so I fail to complete the goal that I set for myself.

A few years ago my family joined a local Tae Kwon Do studio. Over the course of the past three years we have all progressed through the ranks . . . from white, to yellow, to red, and finally to black belts. If you've been a student of martial arts, you know that earning your first black belt is a milestone indicating that you've mastered the basic levels of the art. But the reality is that the real journey of martial arts BEGINS with a Level 1 first degree black belt. One of my goals this year is to earn my second degree black belt.

To meet this goal will require a lot of hard work, many studio sessions and the better part of the year to complete. In my younger days my goal setting would list the number of classes that I needed to attend, and the frequency of testing required to earn this new award. Unfortunately this method of goal setting usually failed to keep me motivated for the year.

Instead of simply listing "tasks" as my goals, I VISUALIZE

what I want the end-result to look like. What does my level of physical endurance need to look like? How high do I need to jump when doing sidekicks? How many boards do I need to be able to break?

Can I see myself doing each of these things? (Unfortunately, in my current shape, no). This year I've gained a few pounds and lost a lot of endurance that I built up from jogging on a regular basis. Now I need to visualize a different person. The person I want to be looks a lot different; for starters, he's about 10 to 20 pounds lighter.

My desire this year is to LOOK like the martial artist that I see in my vision. Now that will keep me motivated for the whole year. It will also keep me focused on the goal of becoming what I SEE in my dream when I am tempted to keep walking past the treadmill and skip the Tae Kwon Do class.

DISNEYLAND

"Who hasn't been to Disney World?" is probably a more easily answered question to ask than, "Who has been to Disney World?" In 1998 alone forty-two million people walked through the turnstiles at this well-known theme park in Florida . . . without doubt it is one of the most popular tourist attractions on the planet. Who knows how many millions more have entered there since the day that it was officially opened.

The grand opening ceremony convened on October 1, 1971, with thousands of invited guests attending including Mrs. Walt Disney. Unfortunately her husband Walt was not in attendance; he had passed away before the park was completed.

Someone turned to her and said: "Isn't it a shame that your husband couldn't have lived to see this?" Her 'insightful' 'response was: "Oh, he did see it . . . that's why it's here!"

God created us with the ability to imagine, to see something before it actually becomes reality. To see with our natural eyes is a wonderful gift from God, but so is this creative gift called imagination or vision.

If I say 'big brown bear,' you don't see the words; you see the image of a large, brown, fur-covered animal. Why is that? I think it is because we were made as visually-oriented people by our Creator. Imagination or vision is a very powerful gift. In my opinion it is a rare person who does not think in pictures.

PUZZLES AT M.D. ANDERSON HOSPITAL

My wife, Naomi, and I spent many days in the summer and fall of 2006 in M.D. Anderson Cancer Center, Houston, Texas, as we fought the battle with large B cell lymphoma in her body. During the weeks we were there we spent hours sitting in various clinic waiting rooms before she was seen by various medical doctors and their assistants.

During the first couple of weeks at MDA there were days when our daughter and son-in-law, Cindy and Kermit, were with us. We all wanted to make our 'waiting time' productive; so, one of the ways Kermit found to use his time wisely was to work on jigsaw puzzles that someone had already begun. It seems that every waiting room there had a table with such puzzles on them.

Putting together jigsaw puzzles is not my thing! I would much rather read a good book. Although Kermit enjoys a good book, too, from time to time he seemed to enjoy spending time at a table where several items existed: a partially completed puzzle, hundreds of pieces yet to be placed into the puzzle, and most importantly, the puzzle box top showing the picture of the completed puzzle.

Of course, the challenge was to place each piece correctly in the puzzle in order to complete the picture as seen on the box top. Without that picture plainly in view, the whole project would have been useless. The picture on the box top was the 'vision' of the end product.

Vision and VisualiZing is absolutely necessary to 'bring about' any project of any kind. We must see the end from the beginning! How will the completed project look? Seeing that first, guarantees satisfaction later.

Someone has called vision and VisualiZing a mental blueprint.' Someone else has said that it is 'a sanctified dream of the future.' Another has called it 'foresight with insight based on hindsight.'

For those of us who desire to be used of God, fulfilling His purpose for our lives, vision is the 'capacity to allow God's creative powers to create within us dreams and plans for the future. It is conceiving through imagination internally with 'eyes of faith' before one can see reality externally with 'eyes of fact.' While some have called the process of vision 'imagineering' and others have termed it 'visioneering,' we are now calling it 'VisualiZing!'

The Bible says in Proverbs 29:18: "Where there is no vision the people perish." In other words, true living is vitally dependent upon vision. No vision; no vibrancy! Without a vision, a dream, an enlightened revelation . . . people will perish . . . they will be released from productive restraints. But where vision exists, so does the possibility of maximized 'people productivity.'

CREATE THE STEPS FROM THE VISION

It is more important for you to fully understand the destination in your mind's eye than the steps of the process that it will take to get there.

When I am working with clients, I will often ask them to visualize an auditorium. This auditorium is full of your friends and family and everyone is focused on you. Today is the day that you are going to be honored and remembered. Today is your funeral.

Perhaps not the most pleasant visualization, but it is a reality that each of us will face. How will you be remembered? What will your brother and best friend from high-school say? What about your boss or co-workers? What about the people that you haven't yet met, what will they say about you?

BAGS OF SAND

What if you had the job of shoveling sand into burlap bags all day long? Could you be enthusiastic about filling bags with sand and dirt . . . bag after bag after bag, over and over and over again? After filling so many bags, wouldn't you begin to lose excitement? After all, it is back-breaking hard work to shovel sand hour after hour after hour.

But what if you were given this vision: Hurricane Katrina is on her way to your city, New Orleans, and it is imperative that hundreds if not thousands of bags of sand be filled in order to help support the dikes that are all around the city so that the city will not become flooded? Most likely you would now see purpose and meaning to your task of shoveling sand into all of those empty burlap bags. You now have caught the vision . . . VisualiZing the goal is making the difference in your attitude and action.

Vision brings our world into focus. Vision brings order out of chaos. Vision brings significance to otherwise insignificant, thought-to-be-meaningless activities.

'BIG BOAT' BUILDING

Noah wasn't just building a big boat, he was building a ship that would be the 'ark of safety' for all who believed and would enter into it at God's command.

God projected His vision into the mind and heart of His man Noah. Noah caught the vision and proceeded to build according to the 'blueprint' from the Master Architect. Thus, he and his wife and their three sons and their wives were all saved from a 'drowning death' when God 'rained down judgment' on a planet full of vileness and violence.

Sawing gopher wood, hammering it into place, pitching it with pitch inside and outside, and building the three floors of rooms to house a zoo of animals was difficult work. And to think that this assignment lasted one hundred and twenty years before it was completed . . . wow! Yet Noah and his sons never ceased building, because they had 'seen the vision.' They got the picture! It was passed from God to Noah and then from Noah to his sons.

When I speak of 'VisualiZing' the dream, it is more than simply seeing a need or becoming aware of an idea. This is a vision that convicts and convinces you to the point of not only seeing what could be done, but of seeing what *should* be done. This is a vision that *must* happen! This is 'VisualiZing' that grips your soul and thrusts you from placid passivity into energetic activity. It's a vision that demands change!

KING DAVID PRESENTED A VISION

When I read the story of David in II Samuel 5:1-12, I am made to see the development of his vision that excited the people of God both in Israel and in Judah . . . exciting them more than anything that King Saul had ever presented to them! Take note of what that vision did for these Hebrews:

- Vision unites! Notice in verses one through three that 'all the tribes' and 'all the elders' unified behind David.
- Vision provides a place for leadership! In verses four and five we see David reigning and leading both in Hebron and then in Jerusalem.
- Vision commands commitment from its followers! Understand that in verse six through eight David's men rally around the vision and rebuff the contempt of the inhabitants, the Jebusites.
- Vision encourages greatness! Verses nine through ten show us that the dream David had for Jerusalem produced not only a

greatness for him but also for the people who were in agreement with him.

- Vision serves as a magnet drawing others to join the cause! This is seen in verses eleven and twelve revealing that after David conquers Jerusalem, more men decide to join him in establishing the kingdom.

Obviously 'VisualiZing the vision' is an action that births potentiality and possibility. Without it success would not occur!

WHERE AM I GOING?

The story is told of Oliver Wendell Holmes, the late great Supreme Court justice (1841-1935), who at 88 years of age was traveling on a train. When the conductor asked for the ticket from Holmes, he fumbled about for it, but couldn't locate it. He was very upset about this. He searched in every pocket, but no ticket. The conductor, who knew Holmes, said: "it's okay, Judge, we will be glad to trust you. By the time you arrive at your destination, you will probably have found your ticket, but if not, you can mail it to us when you do." But these kind words didn't really help Holmes, who replied: "Sir, my problem is not 'Where is my ticket?' My problem is 'Where am I going?'"

Knowing where you are going, knowing which destination is yours is vitally important as you journey along. There's no doubt about that.

'VISIONEERING'

I think that the story of Nehemiah in the Old Testament is one of the best biblical illustrations available showing the importance of 'VisualiZing' the future and knowing where you are going.

Andy Stanley has written an entire book based upon the book of Nehemiah about what he calls 'Visioneering.' In that book he identifies 'building blocks' that brought about Nehemiah's success in rebuilding the walls of Jerusalem.

Here is a brief 'bullet points' presentation of the gist of his premise:

- A vision begins as a concern
- A vision does not necessarily require immediate action
- A vision requires praying and planning
- God will use your circumstances to position you
- What God originates, He orchestrates
- Walk before your talk; investigate before you initiate

- Communicate your vision as a solution to a problem
- Don't expect others to take greater risks than you will
- Respond to criticism with prayer, possibly revisions
- Don't confuse your plans with God's vision
- Visions when refined must basically remain the same
- Visions thrive in an environment of unity
- Never abandon your moral authority
- Don't become distracted
- There is a divine potential in all you envision to do
- At the end of a God-ordained vision is God Himself
- Maintaining vision requires a set of core beliefs
- Visions require constant attention
- Maintaining a vision requires bold leadership

WHY A VISION?

In an article entitled 'Why a Vision?' written by Chris McCall there is a list of a number of reasons why visualizing a vision is a must:

1. *It Clarifies Direction!* 'Look straight ahead and fix your eyes on what lies before you. Mark out a straight path for your feet; then stick to the path. Don't get side-tracked.' (Proverbs 4:25-27 NLT)

2. *It Invites Unity!* 'May God, who gives patience and encouragement, help you live in complete harmony with each other . . . each with the attitude of Christ Jesus toward another.' (Romans 15:5 NLT)

3. *It Facilitates Function*! 'Go and make disciples of all nations.' (Matthew 28:19 NLT)

4. It Enhances Leadership! 'You are the salt of the earth. But what good is salt if it has lost its flavor? Can you make it useful again? It will be thrown out and trampled underfoot as worthless. You are the light of the world . . . like a city on a mountain, glowing in the night for all to see. Don't hide your light under a basket! Instead, put it on a stand and let it shine for all. In the same way, let your good deeds shine out for all to see, so that everyone will praise your Heavenly Father.' (Matthew 5:13-16 NLT)

5. *It Prompts Passion*! 'Since we are surrounded by such a huge crowd of

witnesses to the life of faith, let us strip off every weight that slows us down, especially the sin that so easily hinders our progress. And let us run with endurance the race that God has set before us. We do this by keeping our eyes on Jesus.' (Hebrews 12:1-3 NLT)

6. *It Fosters Risk Taking*! 'Then Peter called to Him, 'Lord, if it is really you, tell me to come to you by walking on water.' (Matthew 14:28)

7. *It Creates Energy*! 'They replied at once, Good! Let's rebuild the wall! So they began the good work.' (Nehemiah 2:18 NLT)

8. *It Provides Purpose*! 'Being confident of this very thing, that he who has begun a good work in you will perform it until the day of Jesus Christ.' (Philippians 1:6)

_____

THE PASSION PROCESS

The energy for our own VisualiZing comes from our own God Given passions.

Train up a child in the way he should go **[and in keeping with his individual gift or bent]**, *and when he is old he will not depart from it*
Proverbs 22:6 (Amplified)

We need to recognize in ourselves these "gifts" and "bents" in order to have the energy to fulfill our God-given vision.

As leaders we can also help others discover their passions. My friend Dennis McIntee with Leadership Process (leadershipprocess.com) has a great tool that he uses. Take a few moments to complete this exercise:

1. What am I really good at?
2. What do I most like to do?
3. What do I least like to do?
4. What are my strengths?
5. What are my weaknesses?
6. Am I becoming the person I want to be?
7. What makes me feel most alive?
8. Where do I want to be 5 years from now?
9. Where do I want to be 10 years from now?
10. List three things you've always wanted to do but were afraid to do.

11. How do you feel when you think of things you always wanted to do but were afraid to do?
12. I felt best when I _____
13. I feel worst when I _____
14. Recall the last five times you cried and describe the experiences.
15. Recall five moments when you have been incredibly happy.
16. Take a moment to dream. Then ask yourself If you could have any career in the world, what would it be?
17. When you become the most successful person in the world in that field, what other career will you pursue?
18. List 10 things you like to do?
19. Now list the 10 things in life that you think are of value.
20. Now list the 10 things about yourself that you think are really admirable.
21. What is the single most important element missing from your life?

NOW A DEFINING QUESTION:

Describe what a perfect day in your life would be, a day that would make you incredibly happy. (Imagine the day vividly, where you would be living, with whom you are fellowshipping, what you're doing, how you are earning money, how you are dressed, what you physically look like. Be very specific. Can you describe your office or home on this perfect day? Are you traveling, flying, or driving? The day should include all the elements you need to be happy.)

STOP! *Take your answer to the question above and break it down. Look at your description and list the passions you see in this description!*

List ten things which will make your life and your work ideal...with these accomplished list ten things that will make your life feel full and complete.

1._____

2. _____

3._____

4. _____

5. _____

6. _____

7. _____

8. _____

9. _____

10. _____

Add "ZING" to Your Quest for Maximum Success

After completing the Passion Test, list your TOP 5 below.

1. _____

2. _____

3. _____

4. _____

5. _____

LET'S SEEK FOR VISION FROM OUR LORD!

It may be that He will actually give us vision through 'a vision' much as he did with Daniel, with Saul on the road to Damascus, and with John on the island of Patmos. It is not beyond Him to do that! He is still the God of 'dreams and visions.'

Joel prophesied that in the last days: 'Your old men shall dream dreams, your young men shall see visions.' (Joel 2:28) That same declaration was repeated by Peter on the Day of Pentecost when he declared: 'God has said, I will pour out of my Spirit upon all flesh: and your sons and your daughters shall prophesy, and your young men shall see visions, and your old men shall dream dreams.' (Acts 2:17)

Oh, that you and I would have visions and dreams! May we always actively be 'VisualiZing' the future with the clarity of the Spirit's vision!

Old Testament prophets were often referred to as 'seers '. . . why shouldn't present day men and women of God desire to be the same?

MAKE ME, LORD, A DREAMER

I want to close out my part of this chapter with a poem entitled: 'Make Me, Lord, a Dreamer (For Your Kingdom).' I recently discovered this poem in my files . . . although I don't know the name of the poet, I would certainly give credit to him or her if I did.

> *Make me, Lord, a dreamer for Your Kingdom.*
> *Plant in my heart heavenly desires.*
> *Grant faith that can say, 'Impossibilities shall be'*
> *And vision, lest a world should perish not*
> *knowing Thee.*
>
> *Make me, Lord, a dreamer for Your Kingdom.*
> *I would aspire to greater goals for you, God.*
> *So, cause faith to rise, to motivate each word*
> *and deed.*
> *A faith that's well convinced that Jesus meets*
> *every need.*
>
> *Make me, Lord, a dreamer for Your Kingdom.*

> *Dreams that will change a world that's lost its way!*
> *May dreams that first found their birth in your omnipotence,*
> *Come alive in me . . . becoming reality!*

Be a dreamer! Be a visionary! Be a seer! Let's continue 'VisualiZing' the future that God has for us! He wants us to see His 'Big Picture.' Let's see it with eyes of faith!

But having done that . . . there's more that must be done, or being a 'dreamer' may be nothing more than being a 'daydreamer' who never accomplishes anything. In the next chapter we will consider the next step beyond 'VisualiZing.'

Vic Schober / Jonathan Schober

VERBALIZING: *Saying* Your Ultimate Goal

VerbaliZing: To use words to express or communicate meaning

Any holiday season is a great time to reconnect with friends and family and enjoy the year's blessings. For many of us it's also the time of year when we are planning and setting goals for the year ahead.

This past Thanksgiving I enjoyed talking with my nephew, Christopher Bell. He has an entrepreneurial spirit and is looking at various ways to leverage his video production skills and talents into a successful business.

As we enjoyed second (and sometimes third) helpings of Thanksgiving dinner, we began to talk through some of the steps he would need to develop in order to bring his vision into reality. It always involves a process!

Over the years, there are several goals that my wife and I have verbalized out loud:

1. Owning a pewter-colored Suburban van (and it happened)

2. Having a kitchen in a newer home with a larger, more open feeling (and it happened)
3. Restoring relationships that had been devastated for too long (and it's happening)
4. Becoming debt free (we paid off over $103,000 in debt and became 100% debt free in 2010).

Our VerbaliZing of each of these gave us encouragement and energy to believe that they would come true. And they did!

VerbaliZing your vision accomplishes two things:

1. It provides a platform that allows you to describe the vision in a way that can be understood by others.
2. It gives you the opportunity to have feedback and accountability from others.

Recently Dr. Gail Mathews conducted a research experiment to determine how goal achievement is influenced by communicating your goals to others (VerbaliZing). In her study, 149 participants recruited from businesses, organizations, and business networking groups were asked to develop goals and allowed four weeks to rate their progress and the degree to which they had accomplished their goals.

In the final analysis, "those who **expressed their commitments to a friend** *(verbalized)* accomplished significantly more..."

(http://maximizeothers.com/VerbalizeGoals)

WATCH THE VISION AND MAKE IT PLAIN

"I will stand upon my watch and set me upon the tower, and will watch to see what he will say unto me, and what I shall answer when I am reproved.

And the Lord answered me and said, 'Write the vision and make it plain upon tablets, that he may run that reads it. For the vision is yet for an appointed time, but at the end it shall speak and not lie.'"

These are the words of the prophet Habakkuk who wrote them in the book by his name recorded in the Old Testament in Habakkuk chapter two, verses one through three.

So, what's the message that we are to understand from these thoughts?

I think, simply put, this is the message:

- 'Watch to see'. . . first, catch the vision of the Lord!
- 'Write to say'. . . second, put the vision into words.

In other words . . . VisualiZing then VerbaliZing!

To verbalize is to use words to express or communicate meaning! It's just that simple! Words are vehicles of thoughts. No one can really understand or feel or picture with you anything . . . unless it has been articulated adequately. It must be uttered! It must be spoken or written intelligibly in order that the meaning might be fully grasped by anyone beyond the person with the original dream or vision. God shows it; you see it; you say it to others; they see it.

 A man or a woman with an excellent vocabulary has an advantage. He or she can descriptively describe the vision with words: nouns, verbs, adjectives, and adverbs . . . thus giving details that express to others your thoughts which now 'connect the dots' and 'completes the picture' for them.

So, we now see that the second step in this process that brings maximized success is relating and recounting the vision that has been revealed by the Lord through words of revelation that are spoken/written by you.

There are several different ways to consider verbalizing and articulating this thing called vision or visualization. We will consider two or three ways in this chapter.

GOD'S VISION CONCERNING THE CHURCH

First, let's talk about this VisualiZing and VerbaliZing thing as to how it can affect our lives as believers in God for His purposes.

You have a destiny! God has a plan and a purpose for His church. And it is for you to have life and have that life abundantly. Satan has an alternative plan that he wants for your life. His agenda is to kill, to steal, and to destroy you, so that God's dream for you will never be realized.

Here is what God has envisioned for your lives:

- 'This people have I formed for myself; they shall show forth my praise.'
- 'I have created him for my glory, I have formed him; yea, I have made him for my glory.'
- 'You shall be unto me a kingdom of priests and a holy nation.'

These statements are found in Isaiah 43 and Exodus 19.

Peter wrote in his first letter in the second chapter and ninth verse:

- 'You are a chosen generation, a royal priesthood, a holy nation, a peculiar people; that you should show forth the praises of him who has called you out of darkness into his marvelous light.'

Or as John wrote in the Revelation while he was a prisoner on the Island of Patmos:

- 'Unto him that loved us and washed us from our sins in his own blood, and has made us kings and priests unto God and his Father; to him be glory and dominion forever and ever. Amen.'

Obviously whether it was Isaiah or Moses or Peter or John writing, they all agreed that God has a vision for His people: they are to be priests and kings who bring glory and praise to Him. He saw it and had His scribes write it again and again.

WHAT IS A VISION STATEMENT?

Here is another way to consider VisualiZing and VerbaliZing. Every church, organization, and family should have a 'vision statement' and a 'mission's statement.' This is usually a one or two sentence statement that declares through well chosen words the intentions of the group as to what they see as their purpose and calling and then how they see themselves achieving those aims.

When I became the district superintendent for the North Texas District Assemblies of God in 2003 one of the first events that I convened was a series of meetings that we called 'imagineering sessions.' I invited all of the presbyters of our twenty-one sections plus our district executives and district departmental leaders to join with me at our Lakeview Camp and Conference Center for the first of several meetings to see our future as we focused on God's vision for our district . . . and then to adequately articulate that vision by writing out our 'vision statement' and our 'mission statement.'

After several meetings with these official leaders of our North Texas District, this is what we verbalized on paper:

- The NTD Vision Statement: To see the Great Commandment and the Great Commission effectively lived out through our community of local churches and leaders.
- The NTD Mission Statement: Our mission is to partner with the local church through nurturing and mentoring leaders, providing resources and equipping the church to reach, disciple, and multiply.

We saw the ministers, leaders, and members of our more than five hundred and fifty Assemblies of God churches living out their love for God and for the people of God. We also saw them living out God's love for those who yet needed to know His love and the love of His Church. We believed that it should and could happen through the community of congregations and leaders in North Texas. That was and is our NTD vision.

Our mission statement places the district in partnership with those local churches, those who are on the frontlines of 'battling and building', as to assisting their leaders and their laborers with instruction and with resources so that we can reach, teach, and multiply as God blesses.

CHANGE THE COURSE OF TEXAS HISTORY

Our family has a connection with Texas history. Davy Crockett is my great, great, great, great, great grandfather. Both dad and I are proud Texans who bleed 'burnt orange' and root for America's Team, The Dallas Cowboys.

From 1997-2000, I worked for the Republican Party of Texas as their IT Director. At that time Texas was not the "Red" state that it is now. George W. Bush had just won the governorship, but the state was controlled by the Democratic Party.

Our mission statement at the Republican Party during this time was simple: 'Change the Course of Texas History.'

But by the time I left the Republicans held all the statewide offices, the state House of Representatives, and the state Senate.

Today Texas has some of the strongest Pro-Life legislation on the books and apparently another former governor with presidential aspirations who has a list of conservative accomplishments.

In short, we changed the course of Texas history.

STRATEGIC PLANNING IS SO IMPORTANT

I believe in strategic planning. It is the process of determining organizational identity and developing a proactive, on-going, and effective strategy to see vision fulfilled under the leadership of a well-organized team in partnership with God.

When we began our NTD 'Imagineering' process, we had one of our young credentialed ministers in our district, who is a professional coach, help us to focus our attention together on strategic planning. I am so grateful for Stephen Blandino, who served us well as an excellent facilitator during those sessions. Stephen taught us ten keys to successful planning, which I now list for your consideration:

1. Begin with a vision
2. Verbalize that vision
3. Clarify your core values
4. Identify key result areas (objectives)
5. Capture new ideas
6. Identify roadblocks and available resources
7. Set short-range and long-range goals
8. Implement plans
9. Evaluate progress
10. Improve and refine your strategy

STRATEGIC INITIATIVES FOR LAKEVIEW CONFERENCE CENTER

VerbaliZing is a must! To not write is not right!

I serve on the overseeing board of the Lakeview Camp and Conference Center in Maypearl, Texas, and recently was handed their Initiatives and Strategic Plan for 2015. The director for Lakeview, Jaroy Carpenter, in presenting his plan also gave us a report of what has been accomplished already. The previous year's event guest totals were 31,833 participants in 333 total events. He then gave us the printed report with four categories of accomplishments: (1) improvements, (2) community events, (3) marketing, and (4) future initiatives.

Then under the title of 'future initiatives' he verbalized four different categories: (1) communicate, (2) appreciate, (3) recognize, (4) encourage.

Each of these four categories has from six to nine 'bullet points' to further 'flesh out' the topic that is being considered. I will not list them all for our consideration, but I will list several that were in the 'communicate' portion:

- Advance marketing strategies by targeting specific audiences through cost effective media opportunities
- Connect with state wide church leaders, schools, and other influencers at conventions

- Establish a strong social media presence
- Evaluate and expand websites with added features
- Develop clear vision, team-building strategies and CARE values among staff

These are but five written initiatives among many! The idea, of course, is not only to have a vision for making things better, but to succinctly write and distribute what steps you plan to take to accomplish those goals. See it; say it! Seed it; stay it! Plan your work; work your plan!

As I wrote earlier: To not write is not right! Be wise by . . . VisualiZing . . . then, VerbaliZing . . . before you began ActualiZing!

ACTUALIZING: *Seeding* Your Ultimate Goal

ActualiZing: To make actual or real; to bring into existence or being

Have you ever met a person who has great ideas and big dreams about which he's always talking, but he never accomplishes anything? He's made it past the first two steps, but he's either stuck on "analysis paralysis" or simply doesn't have the discipline to take action.

ActualiZing is the beginning step to turn thought into action. In many ways it is "planting the seed" of the idea that you visualized and verbalized about with others. ActualiZing is what begins to separate the "dreamers" from the "doers."

Sometimes we're afraid to take action because of what others might think. What if it doesn't work out? What if I fail? What if this is just a dumb idea?

The key is to focus on just The Next Step. I understand, some visions like building a house or performing brain surgery need a more complete plan, but most visions just need The Next Step AND when you plan on completing that step.

PLANTING THE SEED

VisualiZing a dream-goal and VerbaliZing that dream-goal often requires no more than one man or one woman who is in the leadership position 'seeing' and 'saying' it. But ActualiZing that dream-goal almost always requires planting the 'seed' in the hearts and minds of many people who hopefully will begin participating with the leader in bringing it to reality.

When we began 'ActualiZing', we are not thinking a solo act . . . but rather an entire band, group, or team action. Thus, we might even call this group the 'dream team.' Nehemiah as an individual was first given the 'vision' by God to rebuild the walls of Jerusalem. It was his responsibility to clearly see it in his mind and then articulate it to the king before he could go further. Once he received the 'go-ahead' to pursue this dream, he next traveled to Jerusalem to view the ruins and personally see the devastation. After that occurred, he was ready to plant the 'goal-seed' with the citizenry of that community as to what could be done if they would all unite together to accomplish one purpose. Then, the next logical step required organizing a team for 'ActualiZing' the dream-goal. As you recall he was successful in organizing and administrating the project to its completion.

TEAM WORK MAKES THE DREAM WORK

It's a one, two, three operation . . . step by step by step! Each step is vitally important, but if this third step is not successful through organization, operation and involvement of many, many people, who may not at first be excited but can be motivated to become so, the project will not happen. Too often without the people who are skilled, dedicated workers becoming active participants, a 'dream-goal' simply becomes nothing more than a 'daydream-goal' or a pipe dream . . . a great idea, but one that is simply a vain hope or an illusion.

But when everybody has the vision-seed planted in his soul and he or she join a team that is challenged and eager to produce fruit . . . anything and everything is possible!

Teamwork is:

- Less 'me' and more 'we'
- The fuel that allows common people to attain uncommon results
- Working together, even when apart
- Dividing the task and doubling the success

SIX QUALITIES OF A HIGHLY EFFECTIVE TEAM

I was recently the guest of David Busch, the CEO of Hawaiian Falls which is a very successful chain of water parks in California and in major cities in Texas. His newest water park has just been constructed in Pflugerville, a city in the Greater Austin area of Central Texas.

David Busch is very committed to raising the spiritual level of the communities where he has his Hawaiian Falls parks and he has emphasized this aspect of the business wherever he goes. There are chaplains hired to minister to the employees; there are Bible studies made available to them weekly; and in addition to these things, he has regular training sessions available to the public with qualified speakers on leadership issues, marriage issues, and so forth.

At one of those recent sessions I heard Don Nava share a very interesting, entertaining, and instructive presentation entitled: *Six Qualities of a Highly Effective Team*.

I do not have the space to include all the information that he shared, but I will list the six qualities for your consideration:

Add "ZING" to Your Quest for Maximum Success

1. Common Purpose
2. Clear Roles of Members
3. Accepted Leadership
4. Efficient Systems
5. Excellent Communication
6. Committed Relationships

Please know that this information plus application will equal transformation for your team.

THINK TEAMWORK...THINK SPORTS

When I think of teamwork, I think of sports teams that must play as a unified team or risk losing the game. Some well known coaches and players have talked about that very thing.

Phil Jackson who was the coach for the Chicago Bulls said: 'The strength of the team is each individual member; and the strength of the individual is the team.'

Michael Jordan who once played for the Chicago Bulls said: 'Talent wins games, but teamwork wins championships.'

Mike Krzyzewski who may be best known for being the coach of the first NBA 'Dream Team' that gained fame at the Olympics in Barcelona, Spain, in 1992, said: 'Teamwork is the beauty of our sport, where you have five acting as one. You become selfless.'

Basketball is not the only sport where teamwork is a must. In baseball it's true, too. The legendary *Casey Stengel* once said: 'Getting good players is easy. Getting them to play together is the hard part.'

Tom Landry, the late outstanding coach for the Dallas Cowboys football team, was asked how to build a winning team. His response was: 'My job is to get men to do what they don't want to do, in order to achieve what they've always wanted to achieve.' Victory at the Super Bowl!

Obviously achieving greatness requires team members to be disciplined—with determined, deliberate, daily, definable actions, always keeping a clear dream-goal in focus.

I have heard this saying since I was a youth, but just because it may have 'long, white whiskers' on it does not make it any less true:

There are three kinds of people in the world . . .

1.   People who make things happen
2.   People who watch what's happening
3.   People who wonder what's happening

A productive and successful team is one full of people who make things happen!

Thomas Edison, the famous genius-inventor of many things including the incandescent light bulb, once was asked: "Why do you have twenty-one assistants on your team?" To which he retorted: "If I could solve all the problems myself, I would." Obviously he knew that no one man can do it all.

James Cash Penny, the famous founder of Penny's, a national chain of department stores, once commented: "The best teamwork comes from men who are working independently toward one goal in unison."

These wise men knew the secret of great success. Teamwork! I like the acrostic that someone put together a few years ago: **T**ogether **E**verybody **A**chieves **M**ore!

If you are a leader in your church, your business, or your family, you must be a team player! Your piece of the pie is important, but only as it relates to the 'whole pie.'

BODY PARTS

Eugene H. Peterson in his book *The Message* paraphrases the words of the Apostle Paul to the church at Corinth written in First Corinthians chapter twelve when he writes: "A body isn't just a single part blown up into something huge. It's all the different-but-similar parts arranged and functioning together."

He goes on to say: "For no matter how significant you are, it is only because of what you are a part of. An enormous eye or a gigantic hand wouldn't be a body, but a monster. What we have is one body with many different parts, each its proper size and in its proper place."

I really like the way he puts it here: "No part is important on its own. Can you imagine Eye telling Hand, 'Get lost; I don't need you'? Or, Head telling Foot, 'You are fired, your job has been phased out'?

The way God designed our bodies is a model for understanding our lives together as a church: every part dependent on every other part, the parts we mention and the parts we don't. When one part flourishes, every other part enters in the exuberance. If one part hurts, every other part is involved in the hurt.

Doug Smith says, "Teams share the burden and divide the grief."

Margaret Carty has written: "The nice thing about teamwork is that you always have others on your side."

When Paul the Apostle was teaching the congregation at Ephesus, he talked about God handing out gifts to the church . . . apostles, prophets, evangelists, pastors, and teachers. Each gifted minister was to work within the framework of the Church, His Body. His desire was that we all move rhythmically and easily with each other, efficient and graceful in response to God's Son, fully mature adults, fully developed within and without, fully alive like Christ.

Teamwork! Yokefellows! Yoked with each other and yoked with the Lord Himself. Jesus said that His yoke was easy and His burden was light. *The Message* says it this way: "Walk with me and work with me—watch how I do it. Learn the unforced rhythms of grace. I won't lay anything heavy or ill-fitting on you. Keep company with me and you'll learn to live freely and lightly." That's found in Matthew chapter eleven.

HORSE PULL

I once read of a 'horse pull' competition out West that caught a lot of attention at the rodeo. Several horses had been eliminated from the contest and now there were only two still in competition. One horse was able to pull 8,000 pounds of weight and everybody cheered. But the final contestant proved to be even stronger and pulled 8,500 pounds. Everybody cheered even louder. Of course, the second horse was the winner.

Someone suggested that they put the two horses together to see what they could pull as team members. It was expected that 16,500 pounds would be the limit, but they were in for a surprise. Before the event was completed they discovered that these two horses together could pull 27,000 pounds. Amazing synergy!

The Greek word 'synergia' means joint work; to work together. *Syn*, together + *ergon*, work, combine to form a cooperative action or force that produces the simultaneous action of separate agencies, which, together, have greater total effect than the sum of their individual effects.

It reminds me of the verse in the Bible that declares one can put a thousand to flight, but two can put ten thousand to flight. The power of togetherness . . . the power of teamwork . . . is amazing . . . or should I write: Ama-Z*ing*!

TOGETHER: 'TO-GET-THERE'

In Mark chapter two we read that Jesus had returned to Capernaum and the word was out that he was back home. Of course, a crowd gathered, jamming the entrance to the house where he was teaching and no one could get in or out. As he was teaching an unusual thing occurred. The roof/ceiling of the house began to be disassembled. Four men steadfastly removed the roofing material in order to lower their paraplegic friend into the room where Jesus was. Soon with a hole large enough to accommodate the paralyzed man on the stretcher these four 'team members' began lowering him from the roof into the room.

You know the story. Upon seeing this great act of working faith, Jesus said: 'Get up. Pick up your stretcher and go home.' And the once paralyzed man did just that—he got up, grabbed his stretcher, and walked out, with everyone there watching him. They rubbed their eyes, incredulous—then praised God, saying, 'We've never seen anything like this!'

Team work! Each man tenaciously held onto his piece of the rope until the project was completed. This was not a job for one man or even two . . . it apparently took four men to achieve success. To get there, four men got together as one . . . one team.

CORDS OF ACCORD

That event reminds me of the time shortly after Saul of Tarsus was converted to following Jesus as the Messiah, the Christ. He was eagerly, passionately teaching in Damascus that Jesus was the Son of God even though many of the disciples were doubtful about his sincerity.

But their suspicions didn't slow Saul down. His momentum was up now and he plowed straight into the opposition. After this had gone on quite a long time, some Jews conspired to kill him. They were watching the city gates around the clock so they could kill him.

This is where great teamwork came into the picture. One night several disciples engineered his escape by lowering him over the wall of the city in a basket. Here is another 'cords of accord' team at work. Like the men who saw the paraplegic healed miraculously, these men saw this recently converted evangelist delivered from certain death . . . by lowering him to safety outside the grasp of those who had plotted to take his life.

We don't know the names of any of these men on

either team . . . maybe that's the way it is supposed to be. It's not credit to an individual, but to the team and the team spirit that really matters. There's so much more that could be done if it really didn't matter who got the glory! The power for victory is found in 'team steam.'

HUR WHO?

Everybody recognizes the name Moses and the name Aaron . . . two men who had much to do with the liberation of the Israelites from Egyptian bondage and establishing the new Jewish nation with Aaron as its first high priest. But if you were to ask most Christians, "Who is Hur?" . . . unless they connected his name with Moses and Aaron . . . they would not know.

You remember it was Aaron and Hur who held up the arms of Moses when the three of them were on the mountain top looking down upon Joshua and the Israelite warriors as they battled against the enemy forces. When the arms of Moses were held high, the Israelites prevailed in battle; but when his arms were lowered, they had to retreat. Obviously it was absolutely essential that his arms would be held up high.

Thank God for a little known assistant named Hur. Thank God for many such team members all across this nation who are fulfilling their calling and their mission by faithfully participating in the position to which they have been called. We may seldom recognize their names, but believe me, they are as important as the 'big names' we all know.

WHEN THERE WAS ROCK 'N ROLL IN JERUSALEM

Lazarus is dead! The sisters are in grief! But Jesus has arrived! Watch: the stage will soon be set for a miracle of mammoth proportions.

He directed some who were standing nearby: "Go ahead, roll away the rock."

They immediately rolled it away. Jesus raised his eyes to heaven and prayed, "Father, I'm grateful that you have listened to me. I know you always do listen, but on account of this crowd standing here I've spoken so that they might believe that you sent me."

Then he verbalized with a shout, "Lazarus, come forth!" And he came out, a cadaver no more, wrapped from head to toe, and with a kerchief over his face.

Jesus said to several of them, "Unwrap him and let him loose."

What an exciting event this was! Note the key personalities: Lazarus, Jesus, and the Father in heaven. Note also the lesser known, not even named personalities, those who rolled the stone away and those who stripped off the wrappings that restricted Lazarus in order to set him free from the grave clothes.

They were all team members! They all had a job to do. Please note that God was so willing to let several 'nobodies' become 'somebodies' in this miracle.

I can hear them now . . . several men who later that day or the next day, saying: "I was one of the team that rolled the rock away" or "I was the one who removed the first few strips of cloth that had Lazarus bound up like a mummy." We don't know their names, but we do know they had an assignment from the Lord that they performed immediately and without hesitation. Good job, guys! Well done!

First, Jesus saw a 'vision' of Lazarus alive not dead! Secondly, Jesus verbalized that vision into reality by calling for Lazarus to come forth! Thirdly, the 'Raise-Lazarus-to-Life' Team 'actualized' it into a completed fact by performing their assigned actions and . . . wow! It all happened to the glory of

God!

I want to see! I want to say! And I want to plant seed that will produce a harvest of good fruit that brings glory to God, don't you? Even if our names never get mentioned, right?

VisualiZing! VerbaliZing! ActualiZing! What an AmaZing plan!

STABILIZING: *Staying* Your Ultimate Goal

StabiliZing: To make firm; to bring stability; to resist fluctuation

There are four phases that every group (or vision) will go through: form, storm, norm, and perform.

- **Form:** The vision is created.
- **Storm:** The process of defining the details and developing the plan. This is usually when you begin to enlist the required team members.
- **Norm:** This is where StabiliZing begins. You must understand the "normal" operating conditions. For financial goals, this may be documenting your normal expenses in a budget (electricity, mortgage, transportation, etc.)
- **Perform:** Only after you've "normalized" (stabilized) the conditions can you begin to perform as desired.

Nobody likes to work in chaos. Yet, many of us fail to complete the work that is required to understand and plan for normal events. How many of us have sat around in early November and with surprise in our voice, exclaimed: "Christmas is in December,

this year."

Christmas is in December EVERY year. That's normal!

SAILING THE HIGH SEAS WITH A STABILIZER

No large ocean-going vessel captain would think of venturing out on the high seas without having a device called a stabilizer. Its purpose, of course, is to steady a ship that may find itself in rough waters due to stormy weather.

Neither should we venture into our future designed and designated by the vision-goal we have visualized without desiring to have the stability and the help of the 'heavenly stabilizer', the Holy Spirit.

The word 'stabile' is defined as 'not easily moved or thrown off balance; firm; steady; not likely to break down, fall apart, or give way; fixed. Not likely to be affected adversely; lasting; enduring; steadfast; dependable.'

Although we as individuals and even sometimes as members of a team are prone to be blown 'off course' by winds of opposition, adversity, or pessimism, we will be able to not only actualize the vision, but also stabilize that vision to its completion through the sustaining power of the Holy Spirit.

IF YOU HAVE THE SENSE OF A GOOSE

The next time you see geese heading south for the winter or north for the summer—flying along in a V formation—please consider what science has discovered as to why they fly as a team in that pattern.

As each bird flaps its wings, it creates 'uplift' for the bird immediately following.

By flying in a V formation the whole flock adds at least 71% greater flying range than if each bird were to fly on its own.

The lesson to be learned is: 'People who share a common vision and sense of community can get where they are going more quickly and easily because they are traveling on the thrust of each other. *Teamwork makes the dream work*!'

When a goose falls out of formation, it suddenly feels the drag and resistance of trying to go it alone—and quickly gets back into formation to take advantage of the lifting power of the team member in front.

The lesson to be learned is: 'If we have as much sense as a goose, we will stay in formation with those who are headed in the same direction. It brings stability all the way there.'

By the way, who do you think gave geese the sense to fly in the V formation? I believe it was and is a gift from the Creator Himself by His Spirit.

'GONE WOBBLY'

The former Prime Minister of Great Britain, Margaret Thatcher, known affectionately as the Iron Lady, popularized an interesting phrase: 'gone wobbly.' It simply means that a person or a group has ceased to be steady, fixed, and dependable.

It can happen! There can be VisualiZing, VerbaliZing, and ActualiZing but if there isn't StabiliZing when 'stormy weather conditions' loom menacingly on the horizon, then it is very possible that things can go 'wobbly.' To do so is to shake or tremble like Jell-O; it's to waver in one's opinions and vacillate.

It takes decisive determination to stay the course! Resolute resolutions! If any vision is to come to completion, we must be committed to StabiliZing it.

In our American English language we have a number of colloquial sayings that illustrate this principle: go all out; go whole hog; stick to your guns; make no bones about it; at any price; rain or shine; sink or swim; do or die; come hell or high water; through thick or thin. All of which means you will not detour; your will not retreat; and *you will not quit*. You will 'hang in there.'

This reminds me of something Charles Swindoll wrote in his book *Growing Strong in the Seasons of Life* in the chapter entitled 'Finishing the Course.'

He passed along the quitter's 'Six Phases of a Project':

1. Enthusiasm
2. Disillusionment
3. Panic
4. Search for the guilty
5. Punishment of the innocent
6. Praise and honors for the nonparticipants

That's the downward spiral that occurs when people decide to quit the project!

PADEREWSKI SAVES THE DAY

Ignace Jan Paderewski, the famous composer-pianist, was scheduled to perform at a great concert hall in America. It was an night to remember—black tuxedos and long evening dresses, a high-society extravaganza. Present in the audience that evening was a mother with her fidgety nine year old son. Weary of waiting, he squirmed constantly in his seat. His mother had brought him to hear the keyboard master in hopes that he would be inspired to practice his own piano lessons; so, against his wishes, he had come with his mother.

As she turned to talk with someone, he slipped away enticed by the bright lights on the stage that revealed the biggest concert grand piano he had ever seen. He climbed up the stairs to the stage and quietly took a seat on that tufted piano stool near the keyboard. He placed his trembling hands on the black and white keys of the piano and began to play . . . 'chopsticks'.

The audience that had been conversing with each other suddenly ceased whispering and became very hushed. What was this they were hearing . . . 'chopsticks'?

Then, they saw him. Some were irritated. Some

said, 'Get that boy away from there.' Some asked, 'Where's his mother?' Somebody else said, 'Somebody stop him.'

Backstage, Paderewski heard what was happening on the other side of the curtain and quickly surmised the scene. Hurriedly, he grabbed his coat and rushed out onto the stage. Without a word of announcement, he put his arms around the small boy and placed his own hands on the keyboard, improvising a countermelody to harmonize with the simple song that the boy was playing.

As the music filled the concert hall, Paderewski kept whispering in the boy's ear: 'Keep playing. Don't quit, son. Keep going . . . don't quit . . . don't stop.'

Just the time we are about to give up and quit . . . our Master will put His arms around us and whisper words just like that . . . 'Don't quit! Don't give up! Don't stop!'

'Let us not lose heart in doing good, for in due time we shall reap if we do not grow weary.' (Galatians 6:9)

These days there is a need for uncommon, unconditional, uncompromising commitment to the purpose and goal that has been set before us and there is no one more capable of helping us achieve that level of commitment than the Holy Spirit.

May I remind you of the famous quote of Winston Spencer Churchill, the former Prime Minister of England during World War II, who challenged his audience:

> 'Never, never, in nothing great or small, large or petty, never give in; except to convictions of honor and good sense! Never yield to force; never yield to the apparently overwhelming might of the enemy!'

Basically it can be condensed to say: 'Never, never, never, never quit!'

MY ONE ASPIRATION

I like the determination of Paul as stated in his letter to the Philippians. In chapter three he declares unashamedly, unabashedly: 'One thing I do—it is my one aspiration: forgetting what lies behind and straining forward to what lies ahead, I press on toward the goal to win the prize.'

There's no 'gone wobbly' in Paul! He made up his mind and he persevered! Absolutely, irrevocably, undeniably, undeviatingly decided . . . it will happen!

The Amplified New Testament (Philippians 3) has Paul saying things like:

- For my determined purpose is
- That I may progressively become more deeply acquainted
- I press on to lay hold of (grasp) and make my own

- Paul saw the vision (dream, goal, aim, purpose) and was not disobedient to it.
- Paul spoke and wrote fervently about the vision; telling it everywhere.
- Paul seized every opportunity to bring that vision into being and existence.
- Paul secured the advancement of it by encouraging others to join the action.
- Paul relied on the Spirit to provide him with strength to continue to completion.
- You and I can do the same thing! 'All things are possible in Christ.'

PERSEVERANCE! KEEP ON 'KEEPING ON'!

What more could he do? He spent his entire life attempting to fulfill the vision. He let nothing slow him down or hinder him from his final shout of triumph:

I have fought the good fight . . .

I have finished my course . . .

I have kept the faith . . .

It took persistent perseverance! It took courageous commitment!

It spite of hindrances, obstacles, hard times . . .

- Five times Paul was whipped across his back with 39 lashes
- Three times Paul was beaten with rods
- One time Paul was stoned and left for dead
- Three times Paul was shipwrecked at sea
- Many times Paul was exposed to life-threatening perils all over the world

But Paul never gave up! He never gave in! He just doggedly continued to give out!

Know this: When you 'catch a glimpse' of the vision that the Lord has for you and your church, or company, or family, you won't want to quit either.

Like Paul you may be betrayed by those you thought were your brothers.

Like Paul you may spend many a long and lonely night without sleep.

Like Paul you may miss many a meal as you continue the struggle.

But like Paul, you will also be able to triumphantly shout: 'Mission accomplished!' And experience the Zing of victorious StabiliZing the vision through perseverance and the power of the Holy Spirit.

POLIO DEFEATED

The scourge of the land (USA) in the 1940's was poliomyelitis. It was brazenly, boldly marching across our nation from coast to coast and border to border and no one seemed able to stop its crippling effects.

I was a six-year-old first grader in San Antonio when polio picked on me and put my young life in jeopardy. It was the spring of 1946 and there was no Salk vaccine available because Jonas Salk had not yet developed the vaccine.

My parents checked me out of school and put me to bed . . . praying that somehow I would be healed and that the effects of polio would not permanently cripple me for life.

I still remember the family doctor coming to our home (it was termed a 'house call'); taking a long needle connected to a syringe; inserting it into my spinal column after cautioning me to be very still; drawing out some spinal fluid for testing; and then leaving me alone in my bedroom to wonder if I would ever run and play again. Those were sobering days for the Schober family.

My testimony is simply this: Although I did have polio, God healed me one day by His divine power! When classes began in September of that year, I was once again vibrantly active as a student in the second grade. To God be the glory!

But my reason for telling you this story is to relate to you another great story . . . one about the perseverance of Dr. Jonas Salk.

His persistence in searching for the cure to polio can be stated in one powerful quotation from the good doctor:

> 'My family didn't teach me in terms of failure. They taught me in terms of experience and what can be learned from it. I just made my 201st discovery. But I would never have made it without the previous 200 learned experiences.'

Salk didn't 'go wobbly.' He and his team persevered! Throughout the process they made 'discoveries' of what wouldn't work and eventually what would work. And because of his and their persistence, literally millions of people who took the Salk vaccine defeated poliomyelitis, the enemy of their physical well-being. I call that Super StabiliZing!

DR. THOMAS STARZLS

Liver transplants are common procedures in most major hospitals across America these days . . . but it has not always been so!

Thomas Starzls became interested in organ transplants when he was a surgery resident in medical school back in the 1950's.

In 1958 he sewed new livers into dogs but all died within two days. In 1959 he found a way to stabilize circulation during those animal surgeries and his canine patients lived one week longer.

In March, 1963, Starzls performed the first human liver transplant, but his patient bled to death. That failure plus the hepatitis epidemic in the 1960's forced his liver transplant program to be abandoned.

But Thomas refused to quit! In 1968 he and his team were able to provide the surgical expertise to bring seven children successfully through a liver transplant operation that produced survival for all seven although four of them died within six months. It was an encouraging advancement in the technique, although not a stellar one.

By 1981, after twenty three years of searching for the key to a successful liver transplant, the Starzls team found success. Nineteen out of twenty-two patients lived for long periods of time.

It had been a difficult 23-year-long season of trial and error . . . there were times that he had been vilified by the medical establishment . . . but he had persevered . . . and now liver transplants are routinely done in hospitals not that far from where you live.

He didn't 'go wobbly' . . . he persevered and stabilized a great addition to the repertoire of medical options for giving additional years of life to patients with diseased livers.

Starzls visualized the possibility of liver transplants. He verbalized it to fellow medical peers; some of whom became believers in his dream. A team was established that set to work seeking to know the proper way to accomplish the goal. They persevered until today that once unique and unusual surgical operation has become quite common place and routine. Aren't you glad that this team applied StabiliZing attitudes that made it possible for our generation to experience another great medical breakthrough that has saved thousands of lives?

GOD HAS A GLORIOUS VISION

God has a vision of a people who would be His people: a chosen generation, a royal priesthood, a holy nation. He declared it through one prophet after another. He planned and provided the Way by which we can be that peculiar people called out of darkness into His marvelous light.

The God Squad: the Father, the Son, and the Holy Spirit went to work (each fulfilling his position on the team) to bring about the plan, the vision. The sanctifying Sovereign, the seeking Savior, and the sustaining Stabilizer became the original Dream Team!

God so loved the world that He gave His one and only Son! Jesus became the Way, the Truth, and the Life giving Himself, His life a ransom for many. The Spirit was sent as the Comforter, the Teacher, and the 'Guide-into-all-truth' in order to stabilize us as we complete our journey from earth to glory.

The plan is, of course, to have a glorious church without spot or wrinkle . . . the church that is the Bride made ready for the Bridegroom Jesus Christ, and the soon-to-be Great Marriage in the heavens where the Father will officiate at the wedding to end all weddings. What a day that will be!

After we experience StabiliZing . . . then what?

FINALIZING: *Settling* Your Ultimate Goal

FinaliZing: to make final; to bring to completion

FinaliZing! The Zing to end all Zings! Everything about the vision will be brought to completion!

The Grand Finale!

God's vision for His Church is finalized like this: "But God, who is rich in mercy, for his great love wherewith he loved us, even when we were dead in sins, has quickened us together with Christ, (by grace you are saved;) and has raised us up together and made us sit together in heavenly places in Christ Jesus: That in the ages to come he might show the exceeding riches of his grace in his kindness toward us through Christ Jesus." (Ephesians 2:6,7)

The Amplified Bibles says it like this: "He did this that He might clearly demonstrate through the ages to come the immeasurable, limitless, surpassing riches of His free grace, His unmerited favor, in kindness and goodness of heart toward us in Christ Jesus."

What a future! What a blessed forever!

May I suggest that you do whatever it takes to be a 'Finalist.' Be among those who finish the race! Be among those who put the finishing touches to the original vision!

MORE ABOUT 'FINALIZING'

Let's talk about some things we can do when we have completed our project . . . the one that began with VisualiZing, which proceeded to VerbaliZing, followed by ActualiZing and StabiliZing.

FinaliZing includes a proper celebration now that the process is complete . . . 'Mission Accomplished!'

We have mentioned twice in this book the work of Nehemiah in rebuilding the walls of Jerusalem. There was so much that we could immolate in his plan of action, including how he beautifully finished it.

RecogniZing! Nehemiah recognized all the people who were involved in the rebuilding of the wall. He listed all their names family by family and even included a census of all their children. That was quite a feat! He made sure that no one would be omitted.

When we have our celebration or open house or day of dedication, we would be wise to also recognize all who have been responsible for bringing the vision to completion. It is so important that gratitude be shown! It may take several pages to include all the participants, but it is well worth the effort. It is the least that can be done . . . because each team member matters.

This is no small task. Every name must be included. Remember that listing names is risky business because you run the risk of leaving someone off. So, when you make the list . . . check it over several times . . . enlist others check it over, too. Be generous . . . even include people who may not have done very much; but if they did something, including their name on the list is wisdom.

MemoraliZing. If people have given financial gifts to assist in paying the expenses of the project, especially if in memory of a loved one who had passed on; their names and the names of the deceased family member should be mentioned. You may wish to have a plaque with their names location in the foyer or atrium.

SpiritualiZing. Nehemiah chose to have a

celebration on a special feast day to acknowledge the goodness of God. They read passages of scripture from the Word of God. They sang songs. They celebrated the occasion with food and drink . . . and even gave gifts to various people. "And all the people went their way to eat and to drink, and to send portions of food, and to celebrate with great joy." (Nehemiah 8:12) It was at this time that it was made known to everybody that 'the joy of the Lord is your strength.'

We, too, should have a dedication celebration if it is appropriate (such as the completion of a building program). Reading selected passages of the scriptures and singing songs or having special vocal or instrumental musical arrangements available is always appropriate.

And we, too, should rejoice and have a party! It is not improper to be merry! Have plenty of food and drinks . . . don't spare expenses . . . it is a time for being generous. Your team members and their families and friends want to remember this occasion as something very special.

Add "ZING" to Your Quest for Maximum Success

The 'Zing'er can possibly be best remembered this way . . . the steps in fully developing the vision are:

First:	**SEE it**	VisualiZING
Second:	**SAY it**	VerbaliZING
Third:	**SEED it**	ActualiZING
Fourth:	**STAY it**	StabiliZING
Fifth:	**SETTLE it**	FinaliZING

May your vision/dream become reality!

About the Authors

VIC SCHOBER

Vic has been involved in both pastoral ministry at the local level as well as administrative ministry on the state level. He has traveled in over forty nations of the world in ministry in churches, camps, conventions, and seminars. He has authored five books, composed many Scripture songs, and had extensive radio and television ministry. He has been married to Naomi for fifty-four years and they have two married children and twelve grandchildren.

JONATHAN SCHOBER

Jonathan spent most of his career in the technology industry. He was the IT Director for The Republican Party of Texas (1997-2000), and spent 10+ years at Dell in enterprise operations and services marketing. His roles have always been leadership...either as a technical team leader or as a project manager working with other cross functional leaders to launch a new service offer. He now devotes his time to coaching, consulting, and speaking. He has been happily married to his wife, Jennifer, for twenty years. Together they have three sons and four daughters who they 'homeschool'.

Learn more at http://MaximizeOthers.com/

www.ingramcontent.com/pod-product-compliance
Lightning Source LLC
LaVergne TN
LVHW021118080426
835509LV00021B/3430